Men, Women, and the Meaning of Marriage

David W. Jones

Veritas Publications

Veritas Publications, Wake Forest, NC.

You may use brief quotations from this resource in
books, articles, reviews, papers, and presentations.
For all other uses, please contact Veritas Publications
for permission. Email us at
information@veritaspubs.com.

ISBN-10: 1077525125
ISBN-13: 978-1077525122

For the Church

CONTENTS

David W. Jones

CHAPTER 1:
INTRODUCTION

As I have taught on the topic of gender roles over the years, I've noticed the tendency of some, especially those who are learning about biblical manhood and womanhood for the first time, to develop an incomplete view of the institution in which gender roles are most clearly seen for the majority of adults—that is, the estate of marriage. To be more specific, I've observed that some come to understand marriage as simply the divinely bestowed playing field on which they have the opportunity (or duty) of exercising their gender roles. While there is some truth to this notion, it is far from a complete picture of marriage. Moreover, such a man-centered view of the nature and purpose of marriage may ultimately handicap its proponents in regard to the manifestation of their gender roles. It is in view of this phenomenon, then, that this short book will seek to explore the meaning of marriage. It is my hope that with a fuller understanding of the nature and purpose of this institution, marriage participants will be better equipped to fulfill the gender roles that are inherent to their nuptial bonds.

Undoubtedly, the surest way to gain reliable information about the nature and purpose of marriage is to go back to the account in the Garden of Eden when the divine institution of marriage was first given to humanity by the Lord. Indeed, a survey of the New Testament reveals that this is the methodology employed by both Jesus and Paul in their teachings on marriage (cf. Matt. 19:4–6; Mark 10:6–9; 1 Cor. 6:16; Eph. 5:31). Moreover, it is quite logical, for only in the pre-fallen creation can one find marriage in its pristine state, before it was affected by sin, shaped by cultural practices, and saddled with the burden of personal emotions and past experiences.

As the story is usually retold, after making all that presently exists during the first five and one-half days of the creation week, on the sixth day God crafted the pinnacle of his creation, man, out of the dust of the ground and called him Adam. One of the first duties that the Lord assigned to Adam was the naming of the animals. While no details of this event are recorded in Scripture, it is assumed that the man completed this monumental task with ease. Yet, after viewing and naming all of his fellow creatures, Adam became aware that the other animals differed from him in one important aspect—namely, they all had a counterpart and he did not. Therefore, with this new knowledge in mind, and perhaps with a growing sense of loneliness, Adam petitioned God for a companion, a suitable helper, one who was like him. The Lord heard the man's request and granted it, creating the woman who was to be named Eve. Eve, then, became Adam's wife in the first marriage.

While this narrative certainly would explain how marriage came to be, there is at least one major problem with the account—that is, it is not biblical. Of course, this is not to say that this story does not contain elements of truth, for it surely does. For example, the Lord did make the man and give him the assignment of naming the animals, a task that Adam dutifully fulfilled. However, a reading of Scripture gives no indication that Adam was aware that his solitary existence distinguished him from the other animals, nor any hint that he was lonely in a deficient sense. Indeed, why would Adam have been lonely? He enjoyed perfect, pre-fallen, unbroken fellowship with God, which certainly would have been a personally fulfilling relationship. Rather, a reading of the biblical text reveals that, before giving the man the duty of naming the animals, it was the Lord who came to Adam of his own initiative, not vice-versa, and declared, "It is not good that man should be alone; I will make him a suitable helper" (Gen. 2:18). God then crafted the woman out of the rib of the man and presented her to Adam, along with the basic parameters of the divine institution of marriage.

Although this nuance in the order of the events that surrounded the bestowal of marriage may seem subtle, it is in fact quite a significant distinction, for one's view of both the reasons for and the source of the institution of marriage will have profound implications for one's understanding of marital ideals and distortions. For example, if marriage is an institution that had its beginnings in the mind of man, and was crafted in order to meet an egoistic need of man, then it may be legitimate to view matrimony as an anthropocentric establishment, and to grant mankind a measure of authority, or at least a voice, in regard to the ordering of the institution. However, if the idea of marriage began in the mind of God, as the Bible indicates, and the institution was graciously given to humanity by the Lord at creation, then one ought to expect the orientation of marriage to be theocentric. Indeed, if this is a proper perspective on marriage, then it is the Lord who has the right to set the parameters of the institution, as well as to hold mankind accountable to His own divine standards. Viewed in this light, when men and women come together in nuptial bonds they do not actually create a marriage, but rather they participate in a divinely ordained institution, conceived of by God in eternity past and incorporated into the created order at its inauguration.

In light of the above described theocentric nature and orientation of marriage, it is possible to make two foundational observations about the institution that are essential to understanding the biblical standards that govern marriage. These two observations, both of which will be explored in detail over the following pages, are: first, in an immediate sense, marriage entails the sanctification of mankind; and second, in an ultimate sense, marriage entails the glorification of God.

CHAPTER 2:
MARRIAGE ENTAILS THE SANCTIFICATION OF MANKIND

While marriage, like every other institution in which man participates, must ultimately entail the glorification of God, in an immediate here-and-now sense, marriage entails the sanctification of mankind (or at least the possibility thereof). As will be explained in this section, this is a deductive conclusion that stems from the account of the bestowal of the institution of marriage in the Garden of Eden. Moreover, the notion that marriage entails the sanctification of mankind is in accord with the idea that marriage is constitutionally theocentric, for while sanctification is a process that directly impacts and benefits man, ultimately it is facilitated by the Holy Spirit, involves man becoming like

Christ, and results in the glorification of God.

God's unsolicited declaration, "It is not good that man should be alone" (Gen. 2:18), must have come as a bit of a surprise to Adam. Indeed, structurally speaking, it should garner the attention of the reader of the book of Genesis as well, for six times prior to His evaluation of Adam's condition the Lord had declared various aspects of His creation "good" (Gen. 1:4, 10, 12, 18, 21, 25), even previously concluding that all that existed, including mankind, was "very good" (Gen. 1:31). Then, in the pre-fallen paradise, the perfect Garden of Eden, with Adam in complete obedience to the Lord, God announced that Adam's condition was in some sense "not good" (Gen. 2:18). What shock these words must have caused. Indeed, this divine evaluation invites the obvious question: What was it about Adam's condition that was not good? Of course, a cursory answer is provided within the biblical text itself—that is, there was something about the man's solitary existence that was not good. In other words, Adam's independent state was in some sense deficient, less than it could otherwise be. It would be better, concluded God, for Adam to have a suitable helper, a marriage partner, a wife.

This divine remedy for the man's situation, however, raises yet more questions, for in what sense was the state of marriage qualitatively better than Adam's pre-fallen, sinless, albeit "not good," condition? Perhaps it would be possible to address this question by focusing on one of the many practical benefits of marriage. For example, it was certainly better for Adam to have a wife, for it afforded him the opportunity to procreate. Indeed, procreation is an important aspect of human existence, as is testified to by the primacy of the divine command to multiply (cf. Gen. 1:28; 9:1, 7), the biblical description of children as a blessing from God (cf. Ps. 127:3–5), as well as the Lord's stated desire for godly offspring (cf. Mal. 2:15). Yet, since the institution of marriage is legitimate without children, and given the fact that procreation is biologically possible (although not proper) outside of the bonds of marriage, is it logical to conclude that Adam's childless state is that which prompted God to declare the man's condition to be "not good"? While possible, this rationale for the creation of Eve and bestowal of marriage is less than satisfying. Moreover, if correct, it would seem to mean that all must marry and procreate in order to avoid a deficient existence. This is certainly a problematic notion in view of the scriptural account of Jesus' incarnation and life-long state of singleness, as well as the single state of others in the Bible, such as the apostle Paul (cf. 1 Cor. 7:8).

Yet, perhaps it was a different practical benefit that made the institution of marriage superior to that of Adam's solitary existence. For example, with a marriage partner Adam would have a legitimate venue for sexual expression, thereby enabling him to avoid the pitfalls of sexual sin. Certainly, this would constitute a better state than the alternative. Indeed, as is recorded elsewhere in Scripture, sexual intercourse, along with its curbing effect upon sexual sin, is both a valid and an important benefit of marriage (cf. Prov. 5:18–19; 1 Cor. 7:1–5). However, since the fall of mankind was still a future event, this rationale for the Lord's critical evaluation of the man's then current condition seems to be both anachronistic and inadequate. Moreover, while this solution is conceivable, given that Adam would not have had to struggle with sexual sin prior to the fall, and since sexual expression is logically possible (although not proper) outside of the bonds of marriage, it does not seem likely that sexual fulfillment alone could adequately explain why God created the woman and presented her to the man along with the institution of marriage.

One other practical benefit of marriage, already mentioned in passing, which could explain how the institution was a remedy for the man's less-than-ideal condition, is that with a wife Adam would have the opportunity for companionship. This solution identifies Adam's solitude itself as that which was in view when the Lord declared the man's status to be "not good." Yet, as was previously noted, this answer seems to be wanting, for the biblical narrative does not reference the man's loneliness, and in his pre-fallen state Adam would have enjoyed the favor of the Lord's satisfying company (plus that of a talking snake!). Moreover, if loneliness is that which marred the man's existence, this could have been remedied by the creation of a male companion, or even by the provision of a non-marital female friend. Both of these arrangements would have provided friendship for Adam under less complex circumstances than those inherent to the institution of marriage. Yet, since neither of these arrangements is the solution that the Lord supplied, it seems that companionship alone cannot be the reason for the creation of Eve. Indeed, it seems that whatever deficiency was in view when God declared Adam's condition to be "not good," it was a state that could be uniquely corrected through the institution of marriage.

In light of the seeming inability of the practical benefits of marriage to explain how the institution could address Adam's deficient existence, it is possible that the main impetus for the bestowal of marriage was not practical at all. Indeed, in view of the aforementioned theocentric nature of marriage, it is conceivable that in creating the woman and in giving her to the man in marriage God's purpose was primarily spiritual, not practical. In other words, in accord with the nature and orientation of the institution, the chief rationale for the Lord's creation and bestowal of marriage may have been to enhance Adam's ability to do that for which he was created—that is, to glorify God and to enjoy Him forever (cf. Isa. 43:7; 1 Cor. 10:31). Glorification of God happens as men are sanctified, and sanctification occurs when men learn truth about the Lord and submit to such knowledge. Further reflection upon this idea reveals that there are at least three aspects of God's character and mission that can be uniquely learned through the institution of marriage.

Shepard (?)

God as Husband

One aspect of God's character and mission that can be learned through participating in the institution of marriage is the relational dynamics of the God/believer union. In fact, the idea that a sanctifying knowledge of the Lord may be gained through the analogous relationship that exists between a husband and wife in marriage, and God and His people in redemption, is a common theme in Scripture. While the Lord employs various analogies in the Bible to reveal Himself and to communicate His mission to the world—such as the shepherd/sheep analogy, the vine/branches analogy, and the cornerstone/building analogy, among others—there is none more prevalent in Scripture than the husband/wife marriage analogy. This can be seen in the Old Testament use of the marital relationship to depict the God/Israel relationship (cf. Song of Solomon; Isa. 49:18; 50:1; 54:4–8; Jer. 2:2, 32; 3:14; 31:32; Ezek. 16:1–14; Hos. 1:1–3:5), the New Testament employment of the husband/wife union to describe the Christ/church union (cf. Matt. 9:15; 22:1–14; 25:1–13; Mark 2:19–20; Luke 5:34–35; John 3:29; Rom. 7:1–4; 2 Cor. 11:2; Eph. 5:22–33; Rev. 19:7; 21:2, 9; 22:17), as well as the many passages in both the Old and New Testaments that invoke the language of sexual sin to describe a breach in the spiritual relationship that exists between God and His people (cf. Isa. 1:21; Jer. 3:1–10; 5:7; 23:14; Ezek. 16:15–43; 23:1–49; Hos. 4:13–14; 7:4; Nah. 3:4; Matt. 12:39; 16:4; Mark 8:38; Jas. 4:4; Rev. 2:22; 17:1–19:2).

One specific aspect of the relational dynamics of the God/believer union that may be learned through the institution of marriage is the concept of God as the husband of His people. In fact, Scripture often uses this image in describing the relationship between the Lord and His followers. For example, when addressing God's people, the prophet Isaiah writes, "For your Maker is your husband, the Lord of hosts is His name" (Isa. 54:5), and elsewhere, when pleading with His bride, God Himself declares, "Return, O backsliding children . . . for I am married to you" (Jer. 3:14). While this revelation is available to any reader of the biblical text, it is only through participating in the institution of marriage that mankind can fully understand the depth of this teaching. To elaborate, when a man feels the natural burden of being a husband in marriage (literally a "house-band"—one who holds a family together), which includes leading, protecting, and providing for his wife, it is then that he can truly appreciate the picture of God as the husband of His people. In other words, it is uniquely from within the institution of marriage that the biblical truth of God as husband can be practically realized and appreciated by marriage participants.

The relational dynamics of the God/believer union become even more evident when in the midst of marital difficulties a husband embraces the biblical teaching that "while we were still sinners, Christ died for us" (Rom. 5:8). It is at such times that passages which call for husbands to display Christ-like love for their wives can have full impact. For example, when his wife went astray, God commanded the prophet Hosea, "Go again, love a woman who is loved by a lover and is committing adultery, just like the love of the Lord for the children of Israel" (Hos. 3:1). Later, perhaps with the Lord's instructions to Hosea in mind, the apostle Paul wrote, "Husbands, love your wives, just as Christ as loved the church and gave Himself for her" (Eph. 5:25). Recognition of the self-sacrifice needed in order to show love for a wife who has gone astray can be incredibly revelatory in regard to understanding the depth of Christ's love for

His bride, the church. While trying circumstances are not pleasant and should not be actively sought, quite possibly it is those who experience marital difficulties who have the greatest opportunity to grasp the full truth of God as the husband of His people. Indeed, just as the only way for a husband to purify an errant wife is through self-sacrificial love, so the way in which Christ made possible the purification of His church was through His self-sacrifice on the cross (cf. Eph. 5:25–28). It is one thing to possess this knowledge in theory; it is another to gain it through the trials of a difficult marriage.

A complement to the relational dynamic of God as husband is the picture of the church as His bride. While this is not a truth about God per se, it is a corollary to the revelation of God as husband, and it informs the church how to interact properly with God. Throughout the New Testament the church is referred to as the bride of Christ (cf. 2 Cor. 11:2; Rev. 18:23; 19:7; 21:2, 9), sometimes even being called the body of Christ (cf. Rom. 7:4; 1 Cor. 10:16; 12:27; Eph. 4:12; 5:29–30; Col. 1:24). Moreover, as the bride, whose body is not her own, the church is frequently described as being under the authority of Christ, who is her head (cf. 1 Cor. 11:3; Eph.

1:22; 4:15; 5:23; Col. 1:18). As with the doctrine of God as the husband of His people, the notion that the church is the bride of Christ is a truth that is accessible to any reader of Scripture. Yet, within the institution of marriage, a wife has a unique opportunity both to understand and to embrace the fullness of this teaching as she submits herself to her husband's servant leadership. Furthermore, this aspect of the relational dynamics that exist between God and His people is available not only to wives through submission, but also to husbands who witness and benefit from such conduct. Indeed, as Peter notes, somewhat remarkably, the actions of a submissive wife are so revelatory in regard to the character and mission of God that an unregenerate husband may be won to Christ "without a word" (1 Pet. 3:1; cf. 1 Cor. 7:16).

One additional aspect of the revelation of God as husband that can be learned through the institution of marriage is the reality of divine jealousy. The Bible repeatedly communicates the fact that God is jealous for both His name and His glory (cf. Exod. 20:5; Deut. 4:24; Isa. 48:11). Scripture even records Moses' command to "worship no other god, for the Lord, whose name is Jealous, is a jealous God" (Exod. 34:14). While the Lord is willing to share and give nearly all of His resources to His people, including the sacrifice of His Son, the one thing that God will not share is His glory. The prophet Isaiah reports the Lord's declaration, "I am the Lord . . . My glory I will not give to another" (Isa. 42:8), and Jesus instructed His followers, "Pray then like this: Our Father in Heaven, let your name be kept holy . . . . For yours is the . . . glory forever" (Matt. 6:9, 13, ESV). Given the primacy of God's glory and name, then, it stands to reason that the Lord would be jealous for His people, for they are created in order to glorify His name (cf. Isa. 43:7, 21, 25; 1 Cor. 10:31). Indeed, this is what Scripture records as in reference to His people God proclaims, "I am jealous for Zion with great jealousy" (Zech. 8:2). Additionally, a host of passages demonstrate the truth that when the Lord's people begin to glorify other gods it is then that His jealousy is most clearly aroused (cf. Deut. 32:16–21; 1 Ki. 14:22–23; Ps. 78:58).

Within the institution of marriage, spouses have the unique opportunity to experience relational jealousy, thereby enabling them to understand the truth of God's husband-love for His people, as well as the intensity of divine jealousy. In fact, the potential for jealousy in marriage is so great that the Old Testament civil law contains procedures for regulating a husband's jealousy toward His wife (cf. Num. 5:11–31). Of course, it is possible to feel and to express relational jealousy outside the bonds of marriage, as well as to experience unrighteous jealousy within marriage. Yet, knowledge of the righteous relational jealousy described in Scripture between God and His people can best be gained through participating in the institution of marriage. Indeed, when marriage partners desire to be with their beloved and to protect the purity of their marital relationship there is great opportunity to learn about the depth of the Lord's love for His people. Viewed from the perspective of marriage, then, passages that detail God's righteous jealousy for His bride—such as Ezekiel chapter 28, Jeremiah chapter 3, the Song of Solomon, and the first three chapters of Hosea—can potentially take on new meaning. This is all made possible through the sanctifying revelation of God that has been incorporated into the divine institution of marriage.

God as Creator

As was discussed earlier, when viewed

solely as an anthropocentric practical event, the act of procreation cannot sufficiently account for the bestowal of the institution of marriage. Yet, when viewed as a theocentric, revelatory tool that God uses to show His character and mission to the world, child-bearing can be rightly understood as a sanctifying component of marriage. As will be explained, the primary aspect of the Lord's character that is manifest through procreation is the revelation of God as creator. This knowledge may be properly viewed as a type of general revelation, for it is a natural occurrence for new parents to begin to ask questions about God and His creation. Of course, since it is biologically possible to bear children outside the bonds of marriage, this phenomena is not limited to the institution of marriage. Yet, since by divine intent and decree procreation is properly located within nuptial bonds, the truth of God as creator that is accessible through child-bearing can best be understood from within the framework of marriage.

The first aspect of God's character that is revealed to the reader of Scripture is the fact that the Lord is a creator, for creation is the first act of God recorded in the Bible. In fact, the opening chapter of the Bible explains in great detail the Lord's creation of all that presently exists, excluding human beings, over a five and one-half day period. Then, after creating the land-dwelling animals on the sixth day, and following brief inter-Trinitarian reflection and dialogue that concludes with the decision, "Let Us make man in Our image, according to Our likeness" (Gen. 1:26), God made man. It is significant that immediately following the creation of mankind, the Lord gave Adam and Eve the command, "Be fruitful and multiply; fill the earth" (Gen. 1:28). Not coincidentally, God repeated these exact words to Noah at His re-creation of the world after the flood (cf. Gen. 8:17; 9:1). This mandate, then, is the prime divine directive, the first command ever given to humanity by the Lord. It was first spoken by God at creation to Adam's family, and then after the flood to Noah's family.

In sum, then, just as the first reported act of God was to create, so the Lord's first command to mankind was to procreate. Through child-bearing, then, mankind acts, in a very tangible way, like God. Such functional image-bearing through procreation can be revelatory, both to marriage partners and to the watching world, and is thus a potentially sanctifying event. Moreover, as spouses procreate—an event that nearly all marriage participants seem driven toward—they experience contentment, for in so doing they fulfill the prime divine directive and accomplish that which they were designed to do. Indeed, perhaps with procreation in view, the apostle Paul appealed to this God-ordained sense of fulfillment as he wrote that in a well-ordered marriage a husband is "the savior [i.e., completer] of the body" (Eph. 5:24), and a wife "will be saved [i.e., completed] in childbearing" (1 Tim. 2:15). Given the fact that God could have unilaterally continued to create mankind in His image, but instead chose to give marriage partners the ability to procreate, this command itself ought to be viewed as a manifestation of God's glory and grace.

A further aspect of the Lord's character that can be learned through procreation is the reality of God's love and care for that which He creates. While the act of procreation itself is joyful (cf. Prov. 5:18–19; 1 Cor. 7:1–5), perhaps divinely designed to be so in reflection of God's joy in creation (cf. Gen. 1:31; Job 38:7; Ps. 104:31; Prov. 8:31), an equally satisfying component of child-bearing is caring for one's offspring. The natural desire of parents to provide for and to protect that which they create can be revelatory in regard to understanding God's love for that which He has made. Indeed, it can be a sanctifying activity for parents to learn the depth of God's love for His creation as they ponder the depth of their own love for their children. Moreover, providing and caring for all that is under one's authority is essential to proper image-bearing, and is an underlying assumption in God's second command to mankind to "subdue . . . and have dominion" over all of creation (Gen. 1:28). Not surprisingly, since ministry leaders are to be reflective of the Lord, faithfully providing for and ordering one's marriage and family life is a requirement for church leadership (cf. 1 Tim. 3:4–5, 11–12; Titus 1:6). In summary, then, just as God is both a creator and a provider, so is man to be a creator and a provider.

Through procreation marriage participants may gain sanctifying revelation of God as creator, yet a corollary to this truth involves those who are created—that is, the children born within nuptial bonds, especially to believing marriage partners. The idea here is that when a child sees a parent properly reflecting the divine image in marriage, it may be so revelatory of God's character and mission that it will aid in the eventual salvation and sanctification of the child. The apostle Paul touched upon this concept as he wrote to the Corinthians, teaching that a believing spouse is not to depart from an unbelieving spouse "otherwise your children would be unclean, but now they are holy" (1 Cor. 7:14). As he addressed the deteriorating state of marriage in post-exilic Israel, the prophet Malachi mentioned this truth, too. In his attempt to elevate the institution of marriage, Malachi appealed to Gen. 2:24 and cited the potentially sanctifying effect of believing parents upon their children, rhetorically asking, "But did He not make them one [flesh], having a remnant of the Spirit? And why one [flesh]? He seeks godly offspring" (Mal. 2:15). Perhaps the effectiveness of this revelation of the Lord to children is one of the reasons why Scripture repeatedly stipulates that marriage between individuals of like faith is the ideal (cf. Ex. 34:16; Deut. 7:1–6; 1 Cor. 7:39; 2 Cor. 6:14). In any event, the sanctifying effect of marriage that comes via the knowledge of God as creator is further evidence for the theocentric nature of marriage.

God as Trinity

Another sanctifying aspect of God's character that can be learned through the institution of marriage is the fact that God is triune. Interestingly, the account of the Lord's creation of all that exists during the first five and one-half days of the creation week does not mention plurality within the Godhead, nor does it contain any explicit reference to gender distinction among the animals. Indeed, that the animals are not described as male and female is surprising given that on the fifth day of creation God commanded the sea creatures and the birds of the air, "Be fruitful and multiply" (Gen. 1:22). Then on the sixth day, after creating the other land-dwelling animals, the Lord declared, "Let Us make man in Our image, according to Our likeness" (Gen. 1:26). The text continues, "So God created man in His own image; in the image of God He created him; male and female He created them" (Gen. 1:28). Immediately thereafter, Scripture reports that God bestowed the institution of marriage upon mankind (cf. Gen. 2:24), transforming the first man and the first woman into the first married couple.

In the creation narrative, there is an unmistakable difference between the phrase

"Let there be . . ." in the first five and one-half days of creation, and the assertion "Let Us . . ." that precedes the creation of mankind in God's image. The explicit reference to male and female in the creation of mankind, which follows the declaration of divine intent to make Adam and Eve as image-bearers, is also noteworthy. In short, the significance of the reference to plurality within the Godhead and to gender distinction at the creation of mankind is this: all of creation was made in order to reflect God's character and mission to the world (cf. Ps. 19:1; Rom. 1:20); mankind, however, was made in order to manifest God's character and mission within the world (cf. Ps. 8:3–8). As was previously discussed, in a functional sense, men and women most effectively accomplish this task through the institution of marriage as they act like God by procreating and providing, for God is both a creator and a provider. As marriage partners manifest God's character and mission, then, and as they contemplate such, they can gain sanctifying truth about the triune essence of the God in whose image they are made.

While there are surely many specific aspects of God's Trinitarian nature that can be learned through the institution of marriage, perhaps the most general truth that can be discovered is the concept of distinction within unity, or what might be called the reality of composite unity. On account of the abstractness of the doctrine, the scriptural teaching that God is three Persons in one Being is certainly a difficult concept (cf. John 1:1; 1 John 5:7–8); yet marriage participants can uniquely gain insight into this truth, for they themselves are two persons who become "one-flesh" through their nuptial bonds (Gen. 2:24; Matt. 19:5; 1 Cor. 6:16; Eph. 5:31). As marriage partners experience their own one-flesh existence, then, and as they meditate upon the reality of such, the composite unity of the Godhead should become less obscure. Indeed, the institution of marriage is likely the most practical and effective teaching aid in Scripture that assists mankind in understanding the truth that God is triune in essence.

Marriage, of course, includes physical unity and thus sexual intercourse (note: since Eve was formed from Adam's rib, men and women already are in essence one-flesh); however, the one-flesh union of marriage involves much more than sexual intercourse. Indeed, as Jesus noted, marriage is a one-flesh union between two individuals whom "God has joined together" (Matt. 19:6). As marriage participants can testify, in addition to physical unity, the one-flesh reality of marriage includes emotional unity as well as spiritual unity (at least for believers). Within marriage this unity manifests itself in a variety of ways, including intimate communication, mutual love, oneness of desires, openness of thought, and sharing of goals—all of which are truths about God as Trinity, too. It is on account of this spiritual and emotional unity that husbands and wives rightly come together in physical unity and, as image-bearers of God, create new life. Moreover, one of the reasons why pre-marital sex and extra-marital sex are immoral may be the fact that such perversions distort the revelation of God as Trinity that is available through the divinely ordained institution of marriage. This may be the case, for sexual intercourse outside of the bonds of marriage entails physical one-flesh-ness apart from an intent to become one-flesh in being.

Another sanctifying aspect of God's triune nature that can be learned through the institution of marriage is the fact that there is headship and submission within the Godhead. This truth is worth mentioning here because its evidence is so clear in Scripture and its implications are so wide-ranging for marriage partners. Although several factors—including abuse, uniformed caricatures, the influence of secular ideologies, as well as sin and pride—have caused some to bristle at the idea of distinct gender roles, the Bible is clear in its teaching: husbands are to love, to guide, and to protect their wives, and wives are to help and to submit to their husbands (cf. Eph. 5:22–33; 1 Pet. 3:1–7). For both men and women these roles can be difficult to apply; yet, it is important that they are embraced, for gender roles can be revelatory in regard to understanding aspects of God's triune nature. To elaborate, Scripture is clear that the Father is the head of the Trinity (cf. John 3:34; 1 Cor. 11:3; 15:28; Gal. 4:4), that the Son is subordinate to the Father (cf. John 3:17; 4:34; 6:38; 8:42; 1 Cor. 11:3; 15:24), and that the Holy Spirit is subordinate both to the Father and to the Son (cf. John 15:26; 16:7, 13–14). As spouses embrace their own constitutional gender roles within marriage, they are better able to understand these truths, as well as to appreciate aspects of the functioning of the three Persons of the Godhead. Indeed, for marriage participants, accepting their own gender roles may become easier in light of the revelation that while the Father, the Son, and the Holy Spirit have differing roles within the composite unity of the Trinity, they are equal in essence. The same is true of husband and wife.

While sanctifying revelation of God as Trinity is available through the institution of marriage, it must be admitted that the analogy between the Godhead and marriage participants is an inexact correlation, for in essence the Trinity is 3-in-1 and marriage partners are 2-in-1. In an attempt to make this analogy more congruous, perhaps some may be tempted to draw parallels between the members of a family: husband, wife, and children, and the members of the Trinity: the Father, the Son, and the Holy Spirit. Yet this, too, produces an inexact correlation, for children are the fruit of marriage, not parties to marriage. Others, perhaps, would argue for allowing three parties into a marriage relationship in order to harmonize the marriage/Trinity analogy. Yet, while the Lord did tolerate the sin of polygamy in the Old Testament, just as He tolerated many other sins, such marriages were never blissful, for to have more than two parties in a marriage relationship is contrary to creational design. Ultimately, however, shortcomings in the analogy between the institution of marriage and the Trinity are not problematic, for a rightly ordered marital relationship is effective in revealing truth about the relationship that exists between members of the Godhead. Moreover, incongruence in the analogy serves as a continual reminder that the Father, Son, and Holy Spirit possess far more unity and diversity than is available in the currently sin-tainted institution of marriage.

CHAPTER 3:
MARRIAGE ENTAILS THE
GLORIFICATION OF GOD

As has been explored in the preceding discussion, in an immediate here-and-now sense, marriage entails the sanctification of mankind. This sanctification comes through the revelation of God's character and mission that is available through the institution of marriage. Given the theocentric nature of the institution, as well as the inevitability of realizing one's own personal deficiencies through the practice of marriage, it is perhaps not surprising to learn that marriage can potentially affect sanctification. Yet, to view personal spiritual growth as the ultimate goal of marriage would seemingly be contrary to the God-centered nature of the institution. Indeed, the process of sanctification ought not to be understood as an inherently anthropocentric activity, for as Scripture clearly teaches (cf. Isa. 43:21, 25), mankind is not sanctified for his own ends. Rather, through sanctification mankind becomes like Christ in order to glorify God. This truth, then, sheds light upon a second foundational observation about the institution of marriage—that is, in an ultimate sense, marriage entails the glorification of God.

The fact that marriage ultimately entails the glorification of God leads to the conclusion that the Lord did not create mankind primarily for fellowship with one's spouse, but rather for fellowship with Himself. In a sense, marriage can be rightly viewed as a tool that God uses both to facilitate His own glory and to prepare mankind for divine fellowship. In short, as has been explained, the institution of marriage is designed to point mankind to God. Marriage is revelatory and, as such, the institution of marriage communicates the gospel. It reveals the truth that God is husband, creator, and Trinity, and that He is crafting a people to be His bride. In getting marriage right, then, mankind experiences peace and contentment, for through the process of personal sanctification and in the glorification of God mankind finds and fulfills the purpose and the goal of life. In getting marriage wrong, however, mankind experiences struggle and disharmony, for he is in a very real sense living and preaching a false gospel. In light of this truth, it is not surprising that Scripture identifies "forbidding to marry" (1 Tim. 4:3) as a mark of end times apostasy. Said differently, if false teachers always distort the gospel, and marriage is revelatory of the gospel, then false teachers will necessarily attempt to redefine the institution of marriage.

The idea that marriage entails the glorification of God helps to explain the biblical teaching that while marriage is designed by God to be life-long, it is not eternal. When asked about marriage in the afterlife, Jesus taught, "Those who are counted worthy to attain . . . resurrection from the dead, neither marry nor are given in marriage" (Luke 20:35; cf. Matt. 22:30). The apostle Paul, too, asserted that death breaks the bonds of marriage (cf. Rom. 7:2–3; 1 Cor. 7:39). When marriage is viewed solely through an anthropocentric lens, this doctrine may seem harsh; yet when understood in light of the theocentric nature of marriage, this teaching is quite logical. Indeed, there will be no need of marriage between human beings in the afterlife for the church will be married to Christ (cf. 2 Cor. 11:2; Rev. 18:23; 19:7; 21:2, 9). It is interesting that the eternal state of redeemed man will be similar, in many respects, to the original state of pre-fallen man before the bestowal of marriage—that is, mankind will be as he once was: residing in paradise, enjoying perfect fellowship with God. Yet, redeemed man will be better off for having experienced redemption and having learned truths about God via the institution of marriage that were not accessible to unfallen mankind.

After studying the parallel truths that marriage entails the sanctification of mankind and the glorification of God, a logical question to ask is: What about the state of singleness? While this topic is somewhat peripheral to the present discussion, it is appropriate and possible to make a few observations that may be helpful in answering questions related to the state of singleness. First, it should be noted that marriage is an institution that is available to all. In His grace, the Lord gave marriage to the entire human race as a creation ordinance. While many will not marry due to lack of opportunity, lack of desire, or a host of other factors, most will eventually participate in the institution of marriage. Second, while Scripture seems to indicate that in certain circumstances singleness can be a curse (cf. Ps. 78:63; Jer. 7:34; 16:9; 25:10), the Bible also identifies a divine gift of singleness (cf. Jer. 16:1–4; Matt. 19:11–12; 1 Cor. 7:7). While this gift is oftentimes feared by those who are not yet married, if singleness is a legitimate divine calling, then there are several truths about this gift that are common to all spiritual gifts. These truths include: those who have the gift of singleness will desire to use it; the Body of Christ should benefit from this spiritual gift; and the gift of singleness, like marriage, will result in the sanctification of mankind and the glorification of God (cf. Rom. 12:3–8; 1 Cor. 12:4–11; 1 Pet. 4:10). Therefore, it can be concluded that no one will be "stuck" with the gift of singleness. Rather, Spirit-filled believers who have this divinely ordained gift will embrace it and joyfully use it for the Kingdom of God.

In conclusion, hopefully this short book has demonstrated to the reader that marriage is far more than a divinely bestowed playing field on which men and women have the opportunity of exercising biblical gender roles. To be sure, the manifestation of gender roles is both an important and an integral component of the institution of marriage; yet, as has been argued above, the institution of marriage is ultimately given for the sanctification of mankind and the glorification of God. Biblical manhood and womanhood, then, ought not to be viewed as an end unto itself, but rather as a means of contribution to the larger end of the advancement of the Kingdom of God. May the Lord find us faithful as we seek this goal.

ABOUT THE AUTHOR

David W. Jones is a professor and author working in the field of Christian ethics. Dr. Jones is currently serving as Professor of Christian Ethics, Associate Dean for Theological Studies, and Director of the Th.M. program at Southeastern Baptist Theological Seminary (Wake Forest, NC) where he has been teaching since 2001. Dr. Jones holds a B.S. in pastoral ministries, an M.Div. in pastoral ministry, and a Ph.D. in theological studies with an emphasis in Christian ethics. Dr. Jones' scholarly interests include biblical ethics, material stewardship (including financial ethics, environmental ethics, and related issues), and topics related to marriage and family life. Dr. Jones serves as a Fellow at the L. Russ Bush Center for Faith

& Culture, and has served as a Research Fellow in Christian Ethics at the SBC Ethics & Religious Liberty Commission.

Dr. Jones is the author of many books, articles, essays, and reviews that have appeared in various academic journals as well as in other scholarly publications and in popular venues. His literary works have been translated into numerous foreign languages. Dr. Jones is a moral consultant and is a regular speaker at academic conferences, professional society meetings, radio and television shows, churches, camps, and other ministry-related events. Additionally, Dr. Jones has experience in pastoral and church-planting ministry, denominational work, as well as Bible teaching and curriculum design. He has served as Associate Editor of *The Journal for Biblical Manhood and Womanhood* and is an article referee for both *The Journal of the Evangelical Theological Society* and for *Southeastern Theological Review*. Dr. Jones also serves as a theological reviewer of manuscripts for a number of Christian publishers. He holds memberships in many theological and ethical organizations.

SCRIPTURE INDEX

1 Peter

1 John

Revelation

Made in the USA
Coppell, TX
18 September 2020

38260063R00030